Before the
WRIGHT
BROTHERS

Before the WRIGHT BROTHERS

DON BERLINER

LERNER PUBLICATIONS COMPANY · MINNEAPOLIS

Page 1: This photograph, later damaged in a flood, shows a typical scene from the autumn of 1902 near Kitty Hawk. Onlookers watch Wilbur Wright (left) and an assistant launch the 1902 glider piloted by Orville Wright.
Page 2: Augustus Herring's triplane glider is in the air, off the dunes of Lake Michigan's south shore.

Library of Congress Cataloging-in-Publication Data

Berliner, Don.
Before the Wright brothers / Don Berliner.
p. cm.
Includes index.
Summary: Describes the ideas and experiments that lead to the
first powered flight by the 1903 "Wright Flyer."
ISBN 0-8225-1588-1
1. Flight—History—Juvenile literature. 2. Airplanes—History—
Juvenile literature. [1. Flight—History. 2. Airplanes—
History.] I. Title.
TL547.B4179   1990
629.133'34'09—dc20   89-31837
                              CIP
                              AC

Manufactured in the United States of America
2 3 4 5 6 - P/JR - 97 96 95 94

CONTENTS

THE DREAM OF FLIGHT

▽

Who knows when a human first dreamed of flying like a bird? The flight of a bird seems so easy, so natural. How frustrating it must have been for humans to have to trudge through forests and up and down rocky mountains while above their heads, birds flew by simply flapping their wings.

If people could fly, they could cross deep gorges and rushing rivers as easily as smooth, level ground. They could escape from predatory animals. They could flee from forest fires.

Humans have strong legs and arms, but they have no wings. No matter how fast they ran, they could not break free of the land. No matter how hard they flapped their arms, they could never rise above the earth. Why is it that the tiny sparrow could do something so wonderful that people could only dream about doing?

Whether early humans realized it or not, they had one advantage which would eventually enable them to fly: a brain with unlimited potential. Although humans were not born with wings, they could figure out how to make their own wings. Since nature failed to show them how to fly, they could teach themselves.

THE FIRST EXPERIMENTERS

Doubtless, many people throughout time have strapped wings to their bodies and jumped from towers or cliffs in an attempt to fly. The first time such an attempt was recorded was in 852 A.D. Armen Firman, a Muslim holy man, put on a huge cloak and jumped from a tower in Spain. Instead of gliding through the air as he expected, he made a parachute-like jump and fell to the ground. It was recorded that "there was enough air in the folds of his cloak to prevent great injury when he reached the ground."

In 1020, a century and a half later, a monk named Eilmer built a set of hand-held wings and jumped off the top of the abbey in Malmesbury, England. He broke both his legs when he landed and was crippled for the rest of his life; all that remains of his attempt is a nearby pub named "The Flying Monk."

There are other tales of attempts to fly that are probably no more than legends. According to a 4,000-year-old Greek myth, Daedalus and his son, Icarus, flew with wings made of feathers that were held together with wax. Icarus flew too close to the sun, the wax melted, and he fell into the sea and drowned.

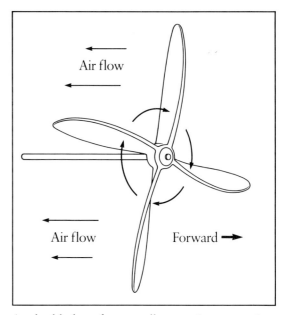

As the blades of a propellor, or airscrew, spin, they push the air backward, like a fan, which causes the propellor and its attachments to move forward.

The first European to think seriously about a piloted flying machine may have been Roger Bacon, a Franciscan monk who lived in England during the 13th century. He believed that if people could build the right kind of craft, the air would support it just as water supports a ship. His writings about ornithopters—aircraft that flew by flapping birdlike wings—led to centuries of attempts to build and fly such machines.

In fact, the simple airscrew principle—used in the Middle Ages in windmills and whirling toys—would be more crucial to the development of powered flight than any wing-flapping machine. As far back as 400 B.C., the Chinese were using the airscrew principle in children's toys. These little spring-powered propellors would fly like modern-day helicopters, straight up for 50 feet (15 meters) or more.

For centuries, the Chinese had used kites to test the winds before setting sail in a ship. By 200 B.C., they had developed kites to the point where they used them to carry information to and from battlefields during wars. They continued to develop kites—using them for signals, playthings, and aerial navigation—possibly to the point where a kite could carry a person.

This engraving of people flying kites in China shows that the Chinese understood—centuries before Europeans—that the kite's rigid wings were the key element to heavier-than-air flight.

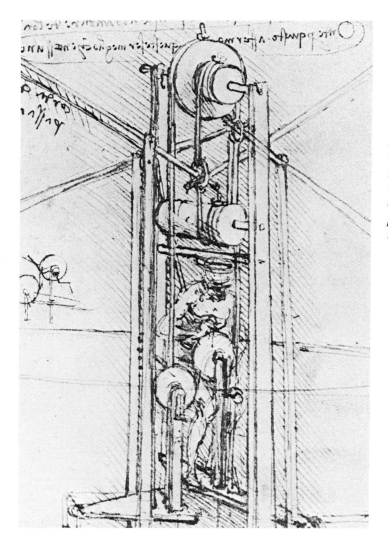

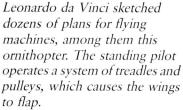

Leonardo da Vinci sketched dozens of plans for flying machines, among them this ornithopter. The standing pilot operates a system of treadles and pulleys, which causes the wings to flap.

Leonardo da Vinci—the artist, musician, architect, mathematician, and scientist—was the first to think about how a flying machine would actually be built. He sketched dozens of propellor-driven helicopters, parachutes, and ornithopters with flapping wings, all complete with diagrams that showed how they were supposed to be built and how they were supposed to operate. Even though most of his ideas would have been unflyable had they been built, Leonardo's ornithopters improved upon Bacon's in one aspect—they were drawn with stabilizing tails. His one workable idea was the propellor-driven helicopter, designed

around the airscrew principle. However, human muscles were not strong enough and there were no engines light enough at that time to provide the power to lift a helicopter and its pilot off the ground.

For 300 years, people continued to talk and sketch and dream about all sorts of strange flying things, including balloons with sails and oars. Then in 1783, a hot-air balloon designed by the Montgolfier brothers lifted off from Paris with two passengers aboard, the Marquis d'Arlandes and Pilatre de Rozier, and flew for several miles before landing safely. The world was astonished, and soon people were flying balloons throughout Europe and the United States.

But a balloon can go only where the wind blows it; it has no power of its own. The controlled flight of birds still frustrated and challenged inventors. They had only to glance out a window to see birds of all sizes taking off, flying in complicated patterns, and then landing on their feet. Why couldn't humans, with all their intelligence and formal education, do as well?

The Marquis d'Arlandes and Pilatre de Rozier, the first humans to fly, wave to a crowd in Paris from their Montgolfier balloon.

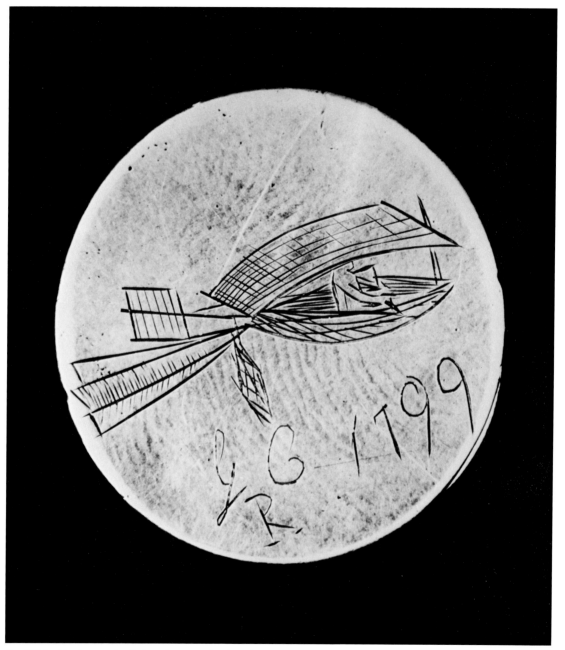

In 1799, Cayley etched the design of a fixed-wing glider on this small silver disc. Cayley was the first European to understand the principles of fixed-wing flight and the necessity of separate control and propulsion systems.

Chapter 1

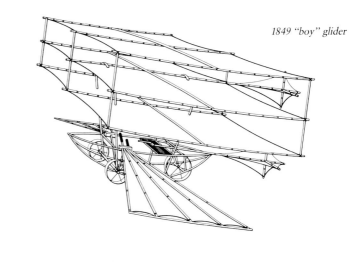

1849 "boy" glider

GEORGE CAYLEY

The first person to make a systematic, scientific study of the design of a fixed-wing airplane was Sir George Cayley, a country gentleman from northern England. Born in 1773, he was a boy when Joseph and Etienne Montgolfier first launched their balloon in France in 1783. All of Europe was suddenly caught up in the excitement of the possibilities of balloon flight. Cayley, however, was more concerned with understanding how birds fly and how people could use the same principles to fly. About 1796, when George Washington was president of the United States, Cayley began to research the science of flight.

By 1799, Cayley had made the most important single discovery in the history of aviation. He found that air flowing over the top of a curved, fixed wing will create *lift*, the upward force that opposes the pull of gravity. Cayley also determined that the larger the wing, and the faster the flow of air over it, the greater the lift that will be created. In addition, he understood the need for some sort of a tail to give an aircraft horizontal and vertical control.

In 1804, when most people were traveling on foot, on horseback, or in a vehicle pulled by horses, Cayley was designing a machine with the potential to fly through the air as fast as 100 miles per hour (161 kilometers per hour). To learn about the sizes and shapes of wings that would work best, he built a "whirling-arm" device, like those used at the time to test windmill sails. Using the whirling-arm device, he was able to learn how some wing shapes allowed air to lift them better than others. From this, he determined that it would be possible to build a wing large enough to lift not only itself but a person as well. Cayley made these experiments the same year the first locomotive was built, long before anyone had invented the automobile or even the bicycle.

Soon after, Cayley built his first model glider, which became the first glider to fly. For the wing, Cayley set a paper kite at an angle on the front part of a pole and a cross-shaped tail on the back part of the pole, which could be moved to adjust the way the glider flew. In his notebook, Cayley wrote, "It was very pretty to see it sail down a steep hill, and it gave [me] the idea that a larger instrument would be a better and safer conveyance down the Alps than even the sure-footed mule."

Sir George Cayley—originator of the airplane

Since the model worked, Cayley began to start work on a glider that would carry a person. In 1808, he even experimented with a lightweight engine powered by gunpowder, but it failed to meet his needs.

In 1809, Cayley designed a full-size glider that could carry a person. There is a possibility that he not only built this machine, but that it made a few short hops piloted by an assistant. Cayley didn't describe the glider in his notebooks, but he did refer to it in his article entitled "On Aerial Navigation," published in 1810. The article dealt with the main problem faced by those trying to design a flying machine: "to make a surface

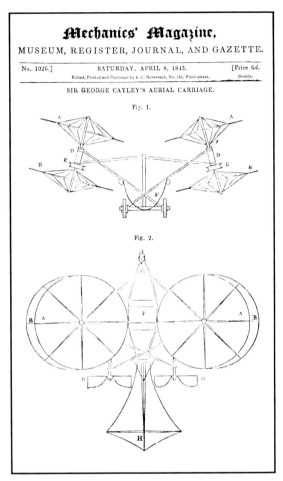

Mechanics' Magazine,
MUSEUM, REGISTER, JOURNAL, AND GAZETTE.

No. 1026.]   SATURDAY, APRIL 8, 1843.   [Price 6d.

Edited, Printed and Published by J. C. Robertson, No. 166, Fleet-street.   Double.

SIR GEORGE CAYLEY'S AERIAL CARRIAGE.

Fig. 1.

Fig. 2.

Cayley's design for a convertiplane

support a given weight by the application of power to the resistance of air." It was the first time anyone had written about the principles of aerodynamics. For the next century, anyone seriously interested in the science of flight would refer to Cayley's writings.

It wasn't until 1849—40 years later—that Cayley is known to have built a large glider. It had *triplane* wings, or three wings in a vertical stack, and two cross-shaped tails on the rear of a simple *fuselage*, or body. Cayley even used at least one wheel for what would later come to be called "landing gear." According to vague reports, the glider rose into the air with a 10-year-old boy on board and flew on its own for a short distance. The boy was almost certainly the first person to fly in a glider, even if he wasn't exactly its pilot.

A few years later, in 1852 or 1853, George Cayley built a single-winged, or *monoplane*, glider that carried a simple three-wheeled cart in which the pilot rode. According to Cayley's notes, it was pulled forward into the air by several people hauling a long rope. It is said to have flown across a valley with Cayley's coachman in the pilot's seat. After it landed, the coachman announced, "I was hired to drive, not to fly!" And he promptly quit driving and flying.

In 1973, a glider just like the one the coachman flew was built for a television documentary about Sir George Cayley. The glider was flown several times, the way it might have flown 120 years earlier. One flight carried the pilot across the same valley, ending with a minor crash. There is little doubt that Cayley's glider designs were flyable. There is no doubt at all that he was the originator of the airplane.

In 1868, Stringfellow's steam-powered model triplane was featured in the first exhibition of the Aeronautical Society of Great Britain, held in London's Crystal Palace. The model never flew.

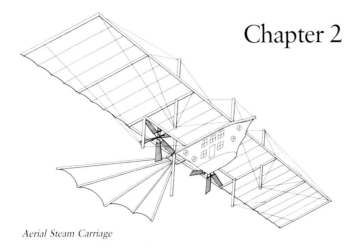

Aerial Steam Carriage

Chapter 2

WILLIAM HENSON
AND JOHN STRINGFELLOW

▽

Sir George Cayley's article, "On Aerial Navigation" was read by Henson and Stringfellow, inventors from England who used the ideas outlined in the article as a basis for their own experiments, developments, and designs in aviation.

William Henson was an engineer who began experimenting with model gliders and small steam engines in 1840. About the same time, John Stringfellow was trying to improve the efficiency of steam engines, which were much too heavy to be used in flying machines.

In 1843, Henson suddenly became famous when his design for a huge "Aerial Steam Carriage" was published in *Mechanics' Magazine*. The steam carriage was a graceful monoplane with a 150-foot (46-m) wingspan, about the same size as a modern 250-passenger DC-10 airliner. Unlike a DC-10, which has engines that produce many thousands of horsepower, the steam carriage's two six-bladed rear propellors were to be driven by no more than a 25-horsepower (17-kilowatt) steam engine designed by Stringfellow.

In this drawing, one steam carriage is flying and another is taking off from an exotic airport.

Even though none of their ideas had been tested yet, Henson and Stringfellow made plans to build many of these enormous flying machines and use them to carry passengers. They formed the Aerial Transit Company and launched a big advertising campaign to raise money for their elaborate plan. Interest in the whole idea soon turned into ridicule, and little money was raised. The company collapsed, partly because it was decades ahead of its time.

This complete failure of the "Aerial Steam Carriage" project forced Henson and Stringfellow to start over, proceeding more cautiously. In 1844, Henson built a large model similar in design to the steam carriage. It had a wingspan of 20 feet (6 m), a boat-shaped fuselage, and two steam-powered propellors at the back of the single wing.

Stringfellow and Henson tried many times between 1844 and 1847 to fly the model, suspending it from an overhead wire until it could get up to flying speed. None of the attempts was successful; the steam engine just wouldn't produce enough power. It was also clear that the model lacked stability, and if it had started flying on its own, it would quickly have gone out of control and crashed. But it was the earliest attempt to build and fly a large, powered model.

William Henson immigrated to the United States in 1848 and ended his research in aviation. John Stringfellow built a new model with 10-foot (3-m) wings, similar to the 1844 model. The improved model had a new steam engine weighing less than nine pounds (4 kilograms). Stringfellow launched it indoors in early 1848 and it flew for an estimated 40 feet (12 m) after leaving the support wire. In August of that year, he flew it outdoors for about 120 feet (37 m), the same distance as the first flight the Wright brothers' *Flyer* would make 55 years later.

Stringfellow lost interest in aviation for many years. When the Aeronautical Society of Great Britain was founded in 1866, he jumped back into aeronautical research and built a triplane model for display in the first Aeronautical Exhibition, held at the Crystal Palace in London in 1868.

The model was tested on a long wire and showed the potential to fly, but it never made a true flight. Stringfellow then began to work on a full-size flying machine that could carry a person, but his eyesight began to fail and he was unable to complete the task.

Even though all the early publicity connected with the "Aerial Steam Carriage" brought ridicule to Henson and Stringfellow, it brought worldwide attention to the possibilities of powered flight. Through their efforts, as well as the work of the new Aeronautical Society, experiments in aviation were seen as less ridiculous and more respectable, paving the way for more aeronautical research.

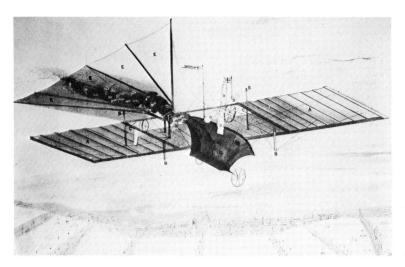

This fanciful drawing, publicity for the Aerial Transit Company, shows the Aerial Steam Carriage soaring over a Far Eastern port.

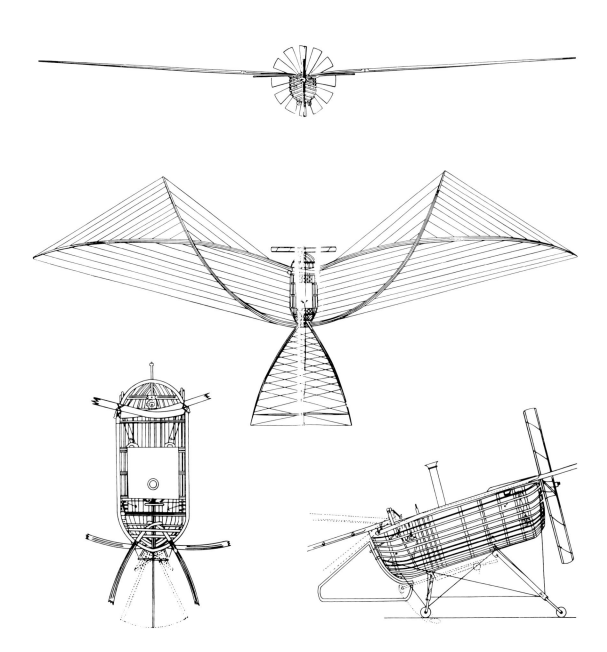

The plans of Felix Du Temple's clockwork-powered monoplane model, which flew in 1857, show the craft from four perspectives.

Chapter 3

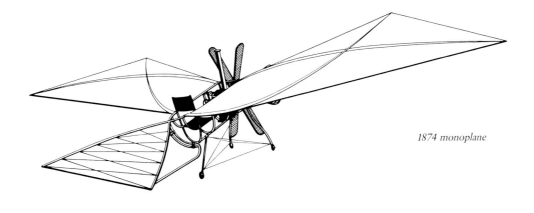

1874 monoplane

FELIX DU TEMPLE

▽

Not all of the attempts to build and fly airplanes were in England. Felix Du Temple, an officer in the French navy, was among those in France who were intrigued by the possibilities of powered flight. Du Temple began work in the middle of the 19th century, and flew a monoplane model powered by a clock-work mechanism in 1857. The design of the small aircraft was quite modern, with its single wing in front and tail behind, and a single propellor in the nose. Even the landing gear was ingenious, with three legs and three wheels like most modern airplanes.

At about the same time, Du Temple received a patent for the design of a piloted monoplane with an upward tilt to the wings. The design for the monoplane also included retractable landing gear, which was to fold up into the fuselage. Both of these ideas, advanced for their time, eventually became commonplace.

For the next 17 years, Du Temple improved his design and searched for an engine that was both light and powerful.

This was one of the biggest problems for aircraft builders at this time. Steam engines were much too heavy, and gasoline engines were still too new to be reliable.

Finally, in 1874, Du Temple's full-size monoplane was finished. It was powered by a hot-air engine that may have been similar to a steam engine. At Brest, in western France, Du Temple towed his monoplane to the top of a 100-foot (30-m) launching ramp. A young sailor under his command was given the "honor" of being the pilot. After the engine was started, the monoplane, with its propellor whirling, slowly began to move forward and pick up speed. It lifted off into the air for a few feet and then plopped down again. The engine just was not powerful enough to keep the small craft in the air.

Felix Du Temple never again attempted to fly, and no one today credits him with achieving more than a very short hop. But his monoplane was the first powered, piloted, fixed-wing craft to hop into the air.

Felix Du Temple

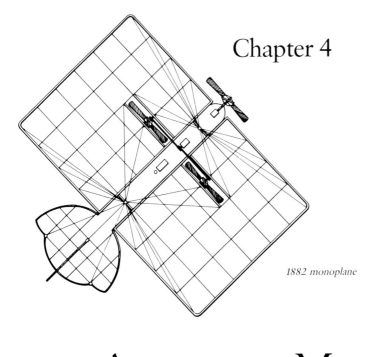

1882 monoplane

Chapter 4

ALEXANDER MOZHAISKI

▽

While most of the efforts to build and fly airplanes were being made in western Europe, at least one person to the east was involved in a long-term scientific study of aeronautics. Alexander Mozhaiski, an engineer and naval officer from St. Petersburg, Russia, began to study the problems of flight in 1856. It wasn't long before he concluded that it really was possible to fly an aircraft, contrary to what most people believed at the time.

Mozhaiski retired from the navy in 1862 to manage his family estate in the Ukraine.

He continued his research, using the works of Cayley and Henson as his guides. He built models to test his ideas for propellors and wings. The results of his tests showed Mozhaiski that the biggest problem was finding a powerful engine. With the right amount of power, he knew that an engine would pull an aircraft forward fast enough for its wing to develop enough lift to raise the aircraft and its pilot from the ground.

In 1879, Mozhaiski traveled to the United States to search for the powerful

In this drawing, Mozhaiski's aircraft is towed into the air by a team of frightened horses.

engine he needed. He failed to find what he was looking for, so he went to England, where he ordered two steam engines: one developing 10 horsepower (7 kw) and another 20 horsepower (15 kw).

From 1880 to 1882 he built his flying machine, the biggest yet. It had a wingspan of 75 feet (23 m) and weighed 2,000 pounds (908 kg), including the fuel and water for the steam engine.

Mozhaiski's aircraft never flew this successfully, but it did lift off briefly before it crashed.

On July 20, 1884, Mozhaiski attempted to fly his machine. With a pilot on board—possibly I. N. Golubev—the aircraft headed down a long ramp, much as Du Temple's had 10 years before. It, too, rose into the air briefly, but it then veered off to one side and crashed into a fence. There are no records of the test to explain why the aircraft crashed, but it probably lacked the powerful controls needed to keep it going straight.

For many years the Soviet government claimed that Mozhaiski's aircraft had made the first successful powered flight, and therefore that a Russian had invented the airplane. The Soviets later retracted that statement and stated only that Mozhaiski built the first aircraft *capable* of flight, and that the Wright brothers were the first actually to fly.

Above: In this photograph, Maxim's huge flying machine would move forward, to the right. The surface pointing upward is the right wing.
Right: Maxim (far right) and two others stand in the cockpit of the "steam kite" after its abortive flight.

Chapter 5

steam kite

Hiram Maxim

---▽---

The first American to seriously think about powered flight, then go on to build a flying machine that would lift off under its own power, was Hiram Maxim, born in Maine in 1840. He started to design a machine gun, but with the lukewarm response the U.S. War and Navy departments gave his invention, he immigrated to England, where the government was more interested in his ideas. In 1884, he perfected the machine gun, becoming rich and famous as a result. He later became a British citizen.

Like the others who had been working on aeronautical research, Maxim spent years studying what had been written about the science of flight. He did many of his own experiments to fill in the large gaps in the knowledge of the subject. Little by little, prospective flyers were becoming more scientific. Maxim was the first to build special instruments that would tell him how his aircraft was working, how much power its steam engines were producing, and how much lifting force its wings were creating.

The biplane Maxim built—he called it a "steam kite" — was a grand contraption. It was about 200 feet (60 m) from tip to tail and towered more than 25 feet (8 m) high. Its wingspan stretched 107 feet (33 m). The huge craft, ready for flight, weighed some 8,000 pounds (3,632 kg) including the crew and the hundreds of pounds of water that would be converted into steam by the pair of 180-horsepower (134-kw) steam engines.

Maxim was smart enough to realize that such a powerful machine could do a lot of damage if it got out of control, and so he built a unique testing rig. The steam kite would run along a special 1,800-foot (549-m) track made of steel rails. Above the steel track was a wooden track, arranged to keep the steam kite from lifting more than a few inches. Thus the machine could fly, but not fly free,

at least until Maxim had carefully tested it and found it to be controllable.

At an estate in Kent, in southeastern England, Maxim began construction of his huge steam kite in 1891. On July 31, 1894, the steam kite was ready for a full-power test carrying Maxim at the controls and two other crew members or passengers. The engines were started and run up to full power while the steam kite was held back, its 18-foot (5-m) propellors churning the air. When it was released, the machine surged forward and in a few hundred feet, lifted off the steel rails. It continued to gain speed and lift until it broke through the wooden guard rails, 600 feet (183 m) from where it started.

Parts of one of the wooden rails smashed a propellor and damaged other parts of the steam kite before the engines could be shut down and the whole thing

The steam kite rests on the steel rails. The outer rails are to keep it from rising too high.

brought to a stop. There was no doubt the steam kite had lifted off and flown for a short distance, thanks to engines that may have produced as much as 400 horsepower (298 kw). But the machine was a wreck. It probably could have been rebuilt, but Maxim realized there was little future in the air for steam power. A steam engine big enough to lift a person for a long flight would have to carry so much water that it probably wouldn't be able to get off the ground. So Maxim began to pursue other interests.

He turned his attention back to aviation in 1910 to build a much more conventional aircraft that never flew and to publish a book about his experiments. Because his machine gun was so valuable to the British military, Maxim was knighted in 1901. He lived until 1916. Later, historians expressed doubt about the 1894 steam kite's claimed power and lifting force, and agreed that it could never have flown far because it lacked the controls needed to keep it on course. Maxim added little to the understanding of powered flight. Even so, the publicity surrounding his tests helped to show the public that although a steam-powered machine would probably never be able to fly, some kind of powered, controlled flight was nearly possible.

Ader's Avion III *is under construction in his workshop in Paris.*

Chapter 6

Eole

CLEMENT ADER

    ▽

Clement Ader, born in France in 1841, was an electrical engineer and inventor who also studied how birds and bats flew. In 1873, he built a glider with wings made from goose feathers. To test his bird-shaped craft, he tethered it to the ground and lay on it as the wind raised it into the air and to the end of its tether. Without further tests on the glider, Ader decided to try powered flight.

Although his glider was decidedly bird-like, and although most inventors were inspired by the flight of birds, Ader turned to bats for his inspiration. His first powered flying machine—which he called the *Eole*, or god of the wind—not only had wings that were shaped like a bat's; they even folded the same way. The *Eole* was surprisingly streamlined for 1890. It was powered by a 20-horsepower (15-kw) steam engine that drove a four-bladed propellor made from bamboo. In many ways Ader's design made sense: it was small, with 46-foot (14-m) wings, and it weighed only a few hundred pounds. But because of the shape of the flying

The Avion III *is displayed in the Grand Palais at one of the early International Expositions of Aerial Locomotion in Paris.*

wing and the lack of a control system, the *Eole* could not possibly have flown long without crashing.

Ader attempted to fly his *Eole* on October 9, 1890, on the grounds of a castle near Armainvilliers, France. He fired up the engine, climbed aboard, and after a short run, the *Eole*, with Ader aboard, was in the air. The *Eole* skimmed along, just a few inches above the ground, for what Ader claimed to be about 150 feet (46 m). For the first time in history, a piloted aircraft had taken off under its own power without the aid of a downhill run, and flown.

The *Eole* flew only once, for it was uncontrollable and certain to crash sooner or later. Ader was happy with the results of his first try, attributing the short flight to the length of the field, and set out to build an improved aircraft. The *Avion II* —"avion" means "airplane" in French— was never completed, but Ader continued to plan and design and experiment for five years and finally came up with his *Avion III*.

The *Avion III* was another bat-winged machine. It was slightly larger than the *Eole*, having a wingspan of 56 feet (17 m), a weight of 850 pounds (386 kg), and two propellors driven by the same type of 20-horsepower (15-kw) steam engine. As before, Ader's aircraft had poor flight controls, which made successful flying impossible. If the *Avion III* tipped or tilted when it got into the air, there would be no way to straighten it out.

Despite the lack of controls, Ader pronounced the *Avion III* ready to fly and transported it to a military field near Versailles, France. A mile-long circular track had been cleared for the aircraft. On October 12, 1897, Ader taxied the *Avion III* around the track, with a man steadying each wingtip to keep the aircraft going in the right direction, since there was nothing but the rear wheel for steering. The men kept pace for almost 1,000 feet (305 m) and then gave up, while the *Avion III* continued around for a full lap. It stopped right where it started, under Ader's control. But the marks of the wheels in the damp clay track showed that while part of the weight of the aircraft had been supported by the wings, at no time did all the wheels stop making tracks.

A second try was underway two days later when a sudden gust of wind tipped the *Avion III* onto its side and stopped it. Again, the rear wheel had left the ground, but there was no evidence that the front wheels had ever lifted off. Clearly, the aircraft had moved forward under its own power for a considerable distance, proving that its engine and propellors worked very well.

Inaccurate accounts of the two flight attempts spread throughout Europe, and Clement Ader was credited with having made the first true flights in a heavier-than-air machine. He claimed to have flown for 1,000 feet (305 m) in the *Avion III* on October 14, 1897, and thus professed to be the first person to make a sustained flight under control. According to a report by the French government, however, Ader's flight was a complete failure. But the official reports of the tests were not published, and the results remained a secret for 13 years.

In 1910, a report was released by the French government that showed Ader's claims to be a total fabrication. Even if his batlike wings had done their job, Ader could never have kept his *Avion III* under control long enough to make a true flight. But for many years after the Wright brothers had made hundreds of flights, Europeans continued to think of Ader as the first pilot of a powered aircraft.

Right: Lilienthal soars in his No. 6 glider during 1893. Below: In 1894, he lands No. 6 at the base of the hill he had constructed near Berlin.

Chapter 7

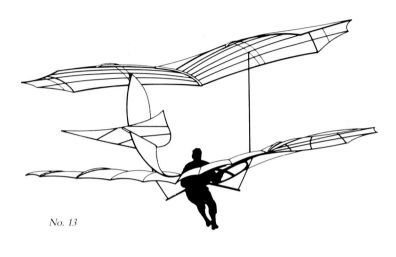

No. 13

OTTO LILIENTHAL

▽

So far, those who were trying to fly heavier-than-air vehicles had built engine-powered machines that were supposed to fly on their first try. So far, this had not worked. These machines lacked balance, stability, and an effective means of control once they were in the air. As a result, no powered aircraft had made more than a short, uncontrolled hop, and no pilot had learned how to fly. In fact, few people realized there was any need to learn how to fly an aircraft. They hadn't thought much past getting their machine off the ground, with a person aboard, and into the air.

The first person to understand that flying an aircraft demanded more than simply taking off was Otto Lilienthal, a talented, systematic experimenter from Germany. Early on, he decided that flying a powered aircraft was beyond his—or anyone else's—knowledge and ability. So Lilienthal set out to learn how to control a flying machine, and thus how to fly.

Lilienthal designed and constructed hang gliders, and starting in 1891, he flew

Children watch Lilienthal as he glides to the earth in his 1895 biplane glider.

them from a hill he had built near Berlin. The first of his hang gliders were monoplanes. Each of them had a hole in the middle of the single wing where Lilienthal held onto the glider while he ran down his hill and jumped into the air. He flew these gliders hundreds of times, rising after a short run and skimming a few feet above the ground for 150 feet (46 m) or more.

With each successful flight, he learned a little more about how to control a glider

Lilienthal soars in one of his early monoplane gliders.

in each of the three dimensions of flight: roll—tipping from side to side; pitch—the nose moving up and down; and yaw —turning right or left. Methodically, Lilienthal developed gliders that were more and more controllable and could be flown more steadily and in stronger winds.

Lilienthal was learning how to fly—the first human to do so. Everyone who had gone before him had made, at best, one or two short hops. No one had been in the air long enough to learn anything about controlling a flying machine. Lilienthal, by contrast, became the first pilot.

In 1895, he built his No. 13 glider, a biplane with a tail in back much like those on modern airplanes. Like his other hang gliders, No. 13 was made from lengths of bamboo that were tied together and covered with cloth. His flights continued to improve and he began to think more seriously about adding a small engine and turning a glider into a powered aircraft.

The next year, he built a complicated glider with four main wings plus a smaller wing above them. He planned to add an engine to this glider to make the wings flap, and the flapping wings would supposedly propel the machine. Unfortunately, a practice flight on August 9, 1896, in one of his monoplane gliders was his last. A gust of wind upset the glider. It stalled, and plunged 50 feet (15 m) to the ground. Otto Lilienthal died in the crash.

Had his luck lasted a little longer, Lilienthal very possibly would have become the first person to fly a powered aircraft. Even so, Lilienthal learned more about how to control and really fly a fixed-wing craft than anyone else who had tried up to that time. And he shared his knowledge with others who were trying to solve the mysteries of flight.

Two newspaper reporters (far right) discover Chanute (3rd from left) and his crew at their camp on the south shore of Lake Michigan in 1896.

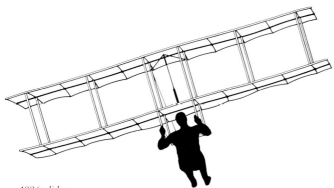

Chapter 8

1896 glider

OCTAVE CHANUTE
AND AUGUSTUS HERRING

▽

One of the biggest problems that the early inventors faced was a lack of information. Although some of the people who were trying to invent a fixed-wing flying machine published their ideas and designs, many others were very secretive, especially about their failures. Consequently, no one really knew what other inventors were working on and what they had already learned. The man who did the most to solve this problem was Octave Chanute, born in France in 1832. When he was six, his family immigrated to the United States. Later, as one of the most talented civil engineers in the country, he moved to Chicago.

In the 1870s, Chanute became interested in aeronautics, collecting all the information he could find on aerodynamics and the history of aeronautical research. He soon began to correspond with experimenters from all over the world, which led him to become a source of information for the latest developments in aviation. In 1894, he published a book entitled *Progress in Flying Machines* that summarized what he had learned. Both Chanute and his book were a great inspiration to people who would become some of the most important in aviation, including Wilbur and Orville Wright.

Octave Chanute had his own ideas for a flying machine, and in 1895, he hired Augustus Herring, a young mechanical engineer from Georgia, to build gliders for him. By this time, Chanute was more than 60 years old and felt he was too old to fly gliders. He preferred to design them and supervise attempts to fly.

Augustus Herring had become interested in aviation in the early 1890s. He built several gliders from plans that Lilienthal had sent him. He made only a few very short flights, but these were enough to attract the attention of Chanute. Soon Herring and two other assistants were building a *multiplane*, or many-winged, glider for Octave Chanute.

In the spring of 1895, Herring left Chanute to accept a higher-paying job working for Samuel Langley at the Smithsonian Institution in Washington, D.C. He worked on steam-powered models of an aircraft that Langley hoped to build in the future. But Herring did not get along well with Langley, and returned to work for Chanute in December 1895.

Chanute and Herring worked hard through the winter of 1896, and by June they had two new gliders ready to be tested. One was a Lilienthal-type glider designed by Herring. The other was Chanute's multiplane. Chanute, Herring, and the other assistants traveled to Miller, Indiana, to test the gliders on the south shore of Lake Michigan.

Several weeks of testing, with the ever-present press looking on, showed them that neither glider flew very well. To control the Lilienthal-type glider, the pilot had to keep his body in the center of gravity by throwing it around in a series of acrobatic movements. After about 100 glides, some of them ending in crashes, the glider was damaged beyond repair. Less than two weeks later, Lilienthal himself was killed in a glider crash in Germany.

Chanute's multiplane, nicknamed the *Katydid*, would not fly farther than about 100 feet (30 m), even though he and Herring tried many different arrangements of the six pairs of wings. Chanute had hoped to achieve automatic stability from the flexible wing joints, which were somewhat like a car's springs. But the wing joints didn't work as well as planned.

After learning as much about aeronautics as they could from the *Katydid*, the group went back to Chicago to modify it into a triplane glider, with three wings in a vertical stack. Unlike the *Katydid* with its movable wings, the triplane had fixed wings. To control the craft, Chanute and Herring added a

Chanute poses with the Katydid, *while Herring (right) and another assistant steady the glider.*

In 1896, the biplane glider made many successful test flights, the longest lasting 14 seconds.

flexible cross-shaped vertical and horizontal tail, which would supposedly make the glider fly more smoothly in rough winds. In late August 1896, they first tested the triplane and quickly decided it didn't need its lowest wing. So they removed the triplane's lowest wing to make it a biplane.

Tests made during September 1896 showed that the new glider was the best yet. One 359-foot (110-m) flight that lasted 14 seconds was better than anything

In October 1896, Augustus Herring returned to the south shore of Lake Michigan with a triplane glider of his own. It had an automatic control system, powered by compressed air, that operated the tail. No one saw Herring's test flights, and so there is a lot of doubt about his claims of having flown as far as 900 feet (274 m). But Herring was convinced that he was on the right track, and so he set out to add an engine to his triplane glider. He had the financial backing of Matthias Arnot, a banker from Elmira, New York, which would later become the gliding capital of the United States.

No more flying took place until September 1897, when Herring began testing a new triplane glider. It was quickly shown to be a success. He flew as far as 600 feet (183 m) and even let newspaper reporters fly it so they could tell their readers what it was like to fly. He was now more convinced than ever that he was ready to fly with power in a flying machine.

A flying machine, with a small compressed-air engine, was ready in October 1898. In it, Herring made two hops, observed by a few onlookers, of about 75 feet (23 m) each. It would seem that this would be just the sort of progress he wanted, and that he should soon be flying longer and longer distances. But Herring's powered glider turned out to be a dead end. It was already too heavy,

achieved by Otto Lilienthal. But while Herring felt they were on the verge of building a successful powered aircraft, Chanute disagreed strongly. He knew there were still major problems to be solved, and he spent the rest of his life spreading information and supporting others.

and installing a bigger engine or adding more fuel would make it still heavier. Like Hiram Maxim and Clement Ader, Augustus Herring had managed to hop into the air but had failed to make a sustained flight.

Before Herring could start to redesign his craft, it was destroyed in a fire. Herring had no money, so he returned to Octave Chanute for work, and became Chanute's representative at the Wright brothers' camp at Kitty Hawk, North Carolina.

There, he realized how much the Wrights had learned in a short time through their painstakingly scientific methods. Herring wasn't heard from again until 1909, when he and Glenn Curtiss—who followed the Wright brothers in aviation research—formed the first aircraft manufacturing company in the United States.

Chanute and Herring's gliders may not have led them to invent the first powered, fixed-wing aircraft, but they did play a major role in the history of aviation. They

showed important aviation pioneers, such as the Wright brothers and Glenn Curtiss, that a biplane with a tail could be flown successfully.

What kept their 1896 and 1897 gliders from being more successful was the necessity of shifting the pilot's position and weight for control. A pilot's movements are sufficient to control small, slow, hang gliders. But they won't provide the kind of control needed for faster, heavier, powered flying machines.

Left: Chanute and Herring search the skies for signs of good flying weather. Center: Herring takes off in his 1897 biplane glider. Right: And soars through the air.

Whitehead and his daughter pose next to his No. 21, a powered monoplane, which he claimed to have flown several times in 1901.

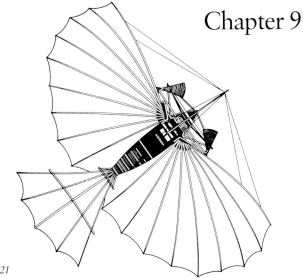

Chapter 9

No. 21

GUSTAVE WHITEHEAD

All of the previous inventors and pioneer aviators tried and, one way or another, failed to make a sustained flight under control. Gustave Whitehead, on the other hand, may have succeeded in truly flying his powered aircraft more than two years before the Wright brothers.

His story is a confusing and controversial one. Many recognized aviation historians consider him little more than a fraud who made big claims but never actually flew. The experts at the Smithsonian's National Air and Space Museum

don't think there's any chance that Whitehead flew. But other people who have studied the evidence are convinced that he flew several times.

Gustave Weisskopf was born in Germany and immigrated to the United States in the 1890s, where he translated his last name into English: "weiss" means "white" and "kopf" means "head." There is no question that he designed and built several flying machines, because photographs and eyewitness testimony have survived. In addition, there are articles from

Whitehead's original No. 21 monoplane is shown from the top. In the 1980s, a duplicate plane was built. Powered by modern engines, it flew.

newspapers from 1900 and 1901 which describe his flying machines and their flights. Unfortunately, not a single photo has been found of a Whitehead aircraft in flight.

Whitehead's most interesting aircraft was the No. 21. He certainly didn't build 20 flying machines before No. 21, but he probably did design that many. The No. 21 had a pair of wings much like those on Lilienthal's monoplane gliders. It had a tail like Henson and Stringfellow's "Aerial Steam Carriage." And its two propellors were in front, just as they are on most modern airplanes. In fact, No. 21's design was much more like modern airplanes than the early Wright brothers' airplanes were.

Whitehead's earliest claim of a true flight goes back to 1899 at Pittsburgh, Pennsylvania. According to a man who swore he not only saw it fly, but flew in it as a passenger with Whitehead, it traveled half a mile at an altitude of nearly 25 feet (8 m). If true, this would have been the first controlled, sustained flight by an aircraft. But only one man's testimony exists, and this isn't enough to convince the doubters.

In 1900, Whitehead moved to Bridgeport, Connecticut, where he continued to work on flying machines. On August 14, 1901, according to the most convincing witnesses, Whitehead flew for about a half mile and as high as 40 feet (12 m) above the ground. An article appeared in the Bridgeport Sunday *Herald* newspaper four days later, written by a reporter who said he saw the flight. It was also reported in two of the most important newspapers of the area: the *Boston Transcript* and the *New York Herald*. Obviously, a lot of people believed that Gustave Whitehead had made this remarkable flight.

Strangely, Whitehead abandoned work on what certainly seem to have been flyable designs, and tried to fly helicopters without any known success. He faded from public view and died in 1927 at the age of 53.

It wasn't until many years later that aviation historians began to investigate his life and work. A few of them came to the conclusion that Whitehead was indeed the first person to pilot a powered, fixed-wing aircraft under control. But they have been unable to convince mainstream historians of Whitehead's importance.

In 1986, several people who lived near Bridgeport decided to find out if his design could have worked. They built a full-size No. 21 aircraft and flew it with the power of two small modern engines. It made many flights and could be maneuvered without crashing. The final step in their task is to fly the No. 21 with a newly-built Whitehead engine.

If the duplicate No. 21 flies with a 1901-style steam engine, it will prove that Gustave Whitehead *could have* flown. But it won't prove that he actually *did* fly, because there is still no solid evidence of his flights. Because it all happened so many years ago, there will probably never be proof that he flew.

Above: In 1903, Jatho's biplane made a short flight. Right: Jatho is tucked into the pilot seat of his 1903 biplane.

Chapter 10

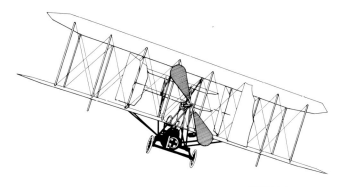

1903 biplane

KARL JATHO

⎯⎯⎯⎯⎯⎯ ▽ ⎯⎯⎯⎯⎯⎯

One of the least known of the early experimenters in aviation was Karl Jatho, a government employee from Hanover, Germany. Jatho's first flying machine was a biplane he built in early 1903. It was just 12 feet (4 m) long and weighed 560 pounds (254 kg), with its main wing on the bottom and a much smaller wing on top. It was powered by a 9-horsepower (7-kw) Buchet gasoline engine, which enabled Jatho to make a "jump flight" of around 60 feet (18 m) on August 18. This wasn't much, but it was a start.

Jatho then redesigned and rebuilt his biplane into a monoplane. It was lighter, at 410 pounds (186 kg), but had less wing area to lift the weight. The engine remained the same 9-horsepower (7-kw) Buchet. Jatho is reported to have flown it several times in the autumn of 1903, his best flight being almost 200 feet (61 m). But his monoplane lacked effective controls. For that reason, his flights were really no more than jumps down a slope, extended by the wings, the rear-mounted propellor, and the engine.

Manly, prepared for a long flight with the compass at his knee, poses with Langley a few days before the Aerodrome was launched for the first time.

Chapter 11

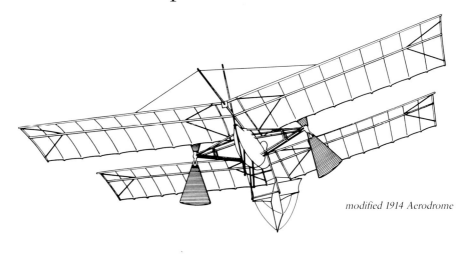

modified 1914 Aerodrome

SAMUEL LANGLEY

▽

The last experimenter to try to fly before the Wright brothers was also the most well known. Samuel Langley was secretary of the Smithsonian Institution and one of the nation's most influential scientists. In 1886, he became interested in mechanical flight and set out to design and build the first heavier-than-air flying machine.

He called all his flying machines "aerodromes," a term he alone used for an aircraft; since 1908, an aerodrome has been defined as an airfield or airport.

Langley's Aerodrome No. 5 was a small scale-model flying machine with tandem wings spanning 13 feet, 8 inches (417 cm). It was 13 feet, 2 inches (401 cm) long, had a total weight of 25 pounds (11 kg), and was powered by only a 1-horsepower (0.7-kw) steam engine.

On May 6, 1896, the Aerodrome No. 5 was launched from a spring-powered catapult on a houseboat on the Potomac River, south of Washington, D.C. The model airplane took off into the wind, climbed to an estimated 100 feet (305 m),

and flew for about 3,300 feet (1,006 m) in graceful curves before running out of steam and landing gently on the water. A second flight, later that same day, lasted a minute and a half, covered 2,300 feet (701 m), and ended just as smoothly, 900 feet (274 m) from where it had started.

These were the first sustained flights by any sort of powered aircraft, even without a person on board. The Aerodrome No. 5 was obviously a stable flyer, thanks to its tandem wings and their upward tilt. There was no way to control the direction it flew, and so the smooth curving of its flight was not a bad sign. Langley was so encouraged by this suc-cess that he built Aerodrome No. 6 and flew it almost a mile on November 28, 1896. He had accomplished what he set out to do: prove that powered flight was possible.

Samuel Langley then retired from aeronautics to concentrate on astronomy, his main interest, and to leave further experiments in powered flight to other people. But war broke out between the U.S. and Spain in 1898, and the U.S. War Department gave Langley $50,000 to build a full-size, piloted Aerodrome that might be useful in the fighting.

Langley's first step was to build a ¼-scale version of the big Aerodrome and to fly it with the power of a gasoline

Langley's full-size Aerodrome is perched on top of a houseboat, ready for launch.

engine. The gasoline engine, although recently invented, offered much greater hope for flight than did the heavy steam engine. Langley immediately went to work on what he confidently felt would be the first piloted, powered aircraft in the world.

The full-size Aerodrome was a big machine. It weighed 730 pounds (331 kg) and had tandem 48-foot (15-m) wings.

The 52-horsepower (39-kw) engine— designed by Stephen Balzer and developed by Charles Manly—was a marvel. It was a radial engine: its five cylinders were arranged like the spokes of a wheel.

Langley planned to launch the big Aerodrome the same way he had launched the models, by catapult from a houseboat moored in the Potomac River. It worked so well for the little ones that

Langley saw no reason to make any changes.

The Aerodrome was mounted on the catapult, more than 20 feet (6 m) above the chilly water. Slung below the fuselage was a crude open compartment for Charles Manly, the pilot. The aircraft had no landing gear of any sort. It isn't clear how it was supposed to land. The models had settled down easily onto the water, but this one would have a human inside. At the very best, Manly would get wet; at the worst, he would drown.

On October 7, 1903, the catapult launched the Aerodrome—with Manly aboard—for the first time. As they cleared the end of the houseboat, something held the Aerodrome briefly. It tilted downward and smacked straight into the water. Manly had managed to pull himself out of the machine as it hit the water and was uninjured. Langley was convinced the aircraft had gotten tangled in the catapult and been pitched into the water by no fault of its own. Others disagree, saying the Aerodrome flatly refused to fly.

The Aerodrome was repaired and on December 8, 1903, Manly climbed into the cockpit again. Once more, the Aerodrome was catapulted forward. This

The Aerodrome is launched from its track atop a houseboat for the first time, the launching mechanism is snagged, and the plane dives into the Potomac.

time the tail collapsed, the aircraft zoomed upwards, turned onto its back, and plunged into the water. Manly got out, but the aircraft was badly damaged as it was pulled out of the river.

No attempts were made to rebuild and fly the Aerodrome because, a few days later, the Wright brothers succeeded in flying four times in a few hours. Langley's ideas were suddenly out of date, though his supporters insisted for many years that he was the true inventor of the airplane.

There is no way to tell how the Aerodrome might have flown if it had been able to survive its launch. But it clearly lacked powerful flight controls. More importantly, it was much too weak to withstand the forces of flight at more than a few miles per hour. Had the Aerodrome started to pick up speed and fly, its undersized main wing spars would surely have snapped in two. Samuel Langley, for all his formal scientific training, did not understand "scale effect," the way a full-size aircraft flies so differently from a ¼-scale model.

Because of his important position in the Smithsonian, Langley was recognized by the Smithsonian as the inventor of the airplane. To "prove" this, the Aerodrome was flown in 1914 by Glenn Curtiss, but it had been secretly modified and was a very different aircraft from the one that had failed so badly in 1903.

After Curtiss modified the Aerodrome's original design and added a new engine, he flies the plane from a lake in New York in 1914.

In 1905, the Flyer III *flies for 20 miles (32 km) in just over 30 minutes.*

Chapter 12

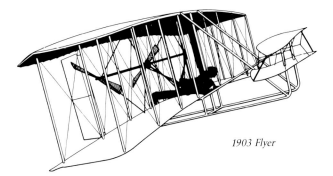

1903 Flyer

ORVILLE AND WILBUR WRIGHT

▽

Between the time Langley flew his scale models and the time his full-size Aerodrome plunged into the Potomac River, two bicycle builders from Dayton, Ohio were busy experimenting with gliders. Wilbur and Orville Wright had first become interested in flying machines as children when their father brought home a whirling toy. Fascinated, they wound up the rubber band on the cork and paper toy to watch it fly again and again. They then built and flew their own versions. Throughout their lives, the brothers experimented with mechanical things; Wilbur would come up with the ideas and Orville would analyze and implement them.

The two brothers opened a shop in 1896 to build and repair bicycles. The same year, Otto Lilienthal was killed when his glider crashed, and the Wrights began to research the problems of human flight. After reading all the information they could find in Dayton, Wilbur wrote to the Smithsonian Institution to ask for all the information it had on aeronautics.

A bicycle built by Wilbur and Orville leans against the fence in front of the Wright brothers' family home in Dayton, Ohio.

The brothers read works by Cayley, Lilienthal's *The Problem of Flying* and *Practical Experiments in Soaring*, Chanute's *Progress in Flying Machines*, and Langley's writings, among others. They discovered that no one had successfully dealt with the basic need for controlling a flying machine.

In 1899, Wilbur and Orville Wright built their first small biplane glider and flew it on a string, like a kite. On this glider, they used their system of "wing warping," which, like ailerons on modern airplanes, changed the angles of the wings. Combined with a stabilizing tail, warping the wings resulted in a relatively controllable aircraft.

In 1900, they built a much larger glider with 17-foot (5-m) wings. Instead of a tail, it had a *rudder*, or moveable horizontal surface, in front of the wings, which would control the up-and-down movement of the nose. The Wright brothers took this glider out to Kitty Hawk, North Carolina, where a strong, steady wind blew over a low hill of bare sand. In October, they began to test it, first flying it controlled from the ground without a pilot, then piloted but tethered, and finally as a free-flying glider. After many flights, and a few crashes, they discovered the rudder helped the horizontal control to such an extent that the pilot could easily land the glider. By the end of October, the Wrights had learned all they could from their 1900 glider and returned to Dayton to design another glider with improvements.

Above: The Wrights' 1900 glider flies from the end of a tether. Right: And then it crashes to the ground. A few days later, the glider was repaired and back on the beach for more tests.

The Wrights' 1901 glider was, like the others, a wire-braced biplane, but it was larger, with a wingspan of 22 feet (7 m) and almost twice as much lifting surface as the others they had built before. They started flying it at Kill Devil Hills, near Kitty Hawk, in July, and it flew so well they were able to make flights of almost 400 feet (122 m) in winds up to 27 miles per hour (43 km/h). They were learning to fly and were well along the way to becoming the first skilled pilots. Even so, as soon as they attempted to make turns, they ran into problems, which persisted into August. Discouraged, the brothers returned to Dayton.

The Wrights began to design their No. 3 glider, which was the largest yet, after extensive laboratory research and experimentation using a wind tunnel—a long box with a fan at one end—to simulate the movement of a wing through the air. The No. 3 glider included the front elevator to control pitch—the nose moving up and down—and the wing warping system to control rolling—tipping from side to side. They added a tail—two fixed, vertical fins at the rear—to prevent turns from becoming spins. The Wrights returned to Kitty Hawk in August 1902 to test it.

Beginning in September, the brothers made almost 1,000 flights with their No. 3 glider. It continued to have problems with turns, so they changed its pair of fixed

fins to a single, moveable, vertical rudder to control yaw—turning right and left. This solved the problem, and the brothers continued to test the glider, making flights of over 600 feet (183 m).

In 1902, Wilbur Wright banks his glider into a controlled turn at Kill Devil Hills.

It may have been that no one else in the world realized that the Wrights had built an aircraft that could be fully controlled and thus genuinely flown. They had learned all of this in no more than one hour of actual piloting. The Wright brothers' next step was obvious: add an engine and turn a fine glider into an airplane. Of course, others had tried this and failed badly. But no one had been as careful and as scientific as Orville and Wilbur Wright. The Wrights had figured out what the problems were, had solved them one by one, and were ready to move ahead now that they knew where they were going.

The 1903 Wright *Flyer* was not a powered version of the 1902 glider, but a completely new machine. It had 40-foot (12-m) wings and a 12-horsepower (9-kw) engine designed and built by the Wrights and mechanic Charlie Taylor. Constructed mainly from spruce and ash and covered with linen, the *Flyer* weighed 750 pounds (341 kg) with its pilot on board. Its two propellors were behind the wing and driven by bicycle chains.

Because of bad weather, the Wright brothers didn't attempt to fly the aircraft until December 14. Wilbur won the coin toss and climbed aboard as the two propellors were swung by hand and the engine started. The *Flyer* raced down the track and shot up into the air so steeply that it stalled and smashed into the sand. Wilbur was not accustomed to working the front rudder with the extra power of the engine and had over-controlled the plane. But they both knew that, with a little practice, they could make their machine fly. Wilbur and Orville packed up their airplane, dragged it back to their simple workshop, and made the needed repairs.

On December 17, the weather was again suitable for flying. Since Wilbur

Wilbur Wright assumes the pilot's position in the 1903 Flyer *just before the first, unsuccessful test flight.*

With Orville in the pilot's position and Wilbur standing by, the Wright brothers successfully make the first controlled flight in a powered aircraft.

had made the first try, it was now Orville's turn. Five observers from the lifesaving station at Kitty Hawk had arrived to watch. The engine was fired up and Orville shook hands with his brother before he climbed into the pilot's position. The *Flyer* moved forward along the track, as Wilbur ran beside it to steady the right wingtip. Orville pulled up on the front rudder, and the *Flyer* lifted up into the air and flew 120 feet (37 m) in 12 seconds.

As Orville later wrote, that flight was "the first in the history of the world in which a machine carrying a man had raised itself by its own power into the air in full flight, had sailed forward without reduction of speed, and had finally landed at a point as high as that from which it started."

In 1895, Otto Lilienthal soars to the earth in his No. 13 glider.

CONCLUSION

△

It took 100 years to bring George Cayley's far-sighted theories to actual human flight in a powered, heavier-than-air machine. Part of the reason was technical and part was personal.

Technically, there were no materials strong or light enough to build a strong, light aircraft that could lift both itself and a pilot. There were no light, powerful engines to pull an aircraft through the air without adding so much weight that it couldn't get off the ground in the first place. None of the work on steam engines helped get a flying machine into the air; it took new ideas about gasoline engines to make powered flight possible.

On a personal level, most people were convinced that humans would never fly. Many people had religious beliefs about what people were created to know and to do. If we were meant to fly, they thought, we would have been born with wings. And so the western world ridiculed the few who tried to fly, and discouraged many others who might have made important contributions.

George Cayley, William Henson and John Stringfellow, Felix Du Temple, Alexander Mozhaiski, Hiram Maxim, Clement Ader, Otto Lilienthal, Octave Chanute and Augustus Herring, Gustave Whitehead, Karl Jatho, Samuel Langley, and Orville and Wilbur Wright were not the only ones who participated in the great experiment to get human beings off the ground and into the sky. But they made the advances in science and technology that eventually led to controllable aircraft. Giving humans the ability to fly has changed our way of thinking, making the entire world more accessible, and bringing all sorts of different people closer together. They made an age-old dream, which had always seemed impossible, possible.

The research and tests conducted by aeronautical scientists, from George Cayley through the Wright brothers, led to advances in technology that have changed our lives. In 1963, a piloted Mercury spaceship lifted off to orbit the earth. Soon humans would fly to the moon, send spacecraft into the solar system and beyond, and dream farther into the unknown than could have been imagined before the Wright brothers.

FOR FURTHER READING

———————▽———————

Berger, Gilda. *Aviation*. New York: Franklin Watts, 1983.

Berliner, Don. *Distance Flights*. Minneapolis: Lerner Publications, 1990.

Briggs, Carole S. *Research Balloons*. Minneapolis: Lerner Publications, 1988.

Dwiggins, Don. *Famous Flyers and the Ships They Flew*. New York: Grosset and Dunlap, 1969.

_____. *Why Airplanes Fly*. Chicago: Children's Press, 1976.

Rosenblum, Richard. *Wings: The Early Years of Aviation*. New York: Four Winds Press, 1980.

The Smithsonian Book of Flight for Young People. New York: Macmillan, 1988.

Williams, Brian. *Aircraft*. New York: Warwick Press, 1981.

In addition, there are books and articles written by George Cayley, Octave Chanute, Samuel Pierpont Langley, Otto Lilienthal, Hiram Maxim, and Wilbur and Orville Wright.

INDEX

Alexander Mozhaiski holds a model of his flying machine. He claimed to have made the first successful powered flight, but he succeeded in only a short, uncontrolled flight.

ACKNOWLEDGMENTS: The illustrations in this book are reproduced through the courtesy of: pp. 1, 15, 58, 60, 61, 62-63, 64, 65, Library of Congress; pp. 2-3, 11, 12, 14, 22, 24, 25, 26, 28, 29, 30, 32, 36, 37, 42-43, 44-45, 50, 52, 54, 55, 56, 57, 66, 71, 72, Smithsonian Institution; p. 6, Florida News Bureau; pp. 7, 8, 13, 17, 21, 23, 27, 31, 35, 39, 47, 51, 53, 59, 67, Laura Westlund; p. 9, Syndics of Cambridge University Library; p. 10, Bibliotheque de l'Institut, Paris; pp. 16, 18, 19, Royal Aeronautical Society; p. 20, Musee de l'Air; p. 34, Deutsches Museum; pp. 38, 41, American Heritage Center, University of Wyoming; pp. 46, 48, Bill O'Dwyer; p. 68, NASA. Cover illustrations courtesy of the Smithsonian Institution (front) and Laura Westlund (back).

Clement Ader claimed to have flown in his bat-winged Avion III, *but he never proved that the craft completely lifted off.*